The Orchard Book of
ROMAN MYTHS

In the same series

THE ORCHARD BOOK OF GREEK MYTHS
Retold by Geraldine McCaughrean
Illustrated by Emma Chichester Clark

THE ORCHARD BOOK OF GREEK GODS AND GODDESSES
Retold by Geraldine McCaughrean
Illustrated by Emma Chichester Clark

ORCHARD BOOKS
338 Euston Road, London NW1 38H
Orchard Books Australia
Level 17/207 Kent Street, Sydney NSW 2000
ISBN 978 1 84362 308 3
First published in 1999 by Orchard Books
This edition published in 2003
Text © Geraldine McCaughrean 1999
Illustrations © Emma Chichester Clark 1999
The rights of Geraldine McCaughrean to be identified as the author
and Emma Chichester Clark as the illustrator of this work
have been asserted by them in accordance with the Copyright,
Designs and Patents Act, 1988.
A CIP catalogue record for this book is available from the British Library.
9 10
Printed in Malaysia
Orchard Books is a division of Hachette Children's Books,
an Hachette UK company.
www.hachette.co.uk

The Orchard Book of
ROMAN MYTHS

Retold by
Geraldine McCaughrean

Illustrated by
Emma Chichester Clark

ORCHARD

CONTENTS

CONTENTS

For Margaret Smith
G.M.

For Will
E.C.C.

INTRODUCTION

The Pantheon in Rome was and is one of the most amazing buildings in the world. For two thousand years its dome was the largest in the world. It needed to be: the Pantheon was a temple dedicated to all the gods of Rome, and the gods of Rome were almost numberless.

Different gods and goddesses controlled every aspect of life: marriage, war, cooking, crops, trade, health, love, fame, doors, latches, hinges, fruit trees, wine … Because the Romans wanted their empire to rival that of Ancient Greece, they deliberately 'imported' the Greek gods and their entire mythology. With typical Roman thoroughness, they even developed a myth tracing their ancestry back to the Trojan Wars: the story of Aeneas.

Their imported gods still lived in Greece, on Mount Olympus … but now, too, at a variety of places around the Mediterranean. And naturally there were also gods and heroes who were uniquely Roman. In fact it became quite difficult for a Roman to remember which of the countless gods to pray to and in which direction to address the prayer. It was safest just to begin: "To whom it may concern, wherever you are …"

One theme recurs again and again in Roman mythology: duty. Such an organised society could never have run so efficiently otherwise: the Romans were fiercely patriotic. They were also savagely superstitious, and spent their lives watching out for omens and staving off bad luck.

Whatever qualities the Roman religion did have, it lacked passion and it lacked any *moral* element. With a person's fate fixed at birth, there was no room for personal goodness, no promise of salvation, no code for living, except a complicated annual round of ritual. As the empire spread – into Europe, into Asia, into Egypt – the occupying Roman soldiers encountered new gods and new myths – Mithras, Isis, and so on – who appealed to their emotions. Eagerly they adopted them. And when Christianity was born within the empire, a fire was lit which would one day burn out the entire pantheon of the gods and convert even Caesar himself to the worship of one god.

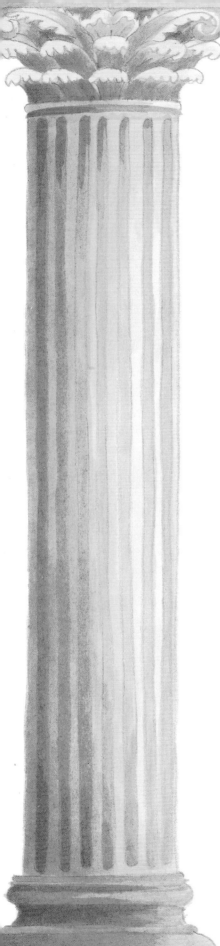

THE OLYMPIANS

*T*he King of the Gods sat on his golden throne, an eagle perched on his shoulder, his feet resting on the world: a picture of glory. The lesser immortals sprawled about the slopes of Olympus, quarrelling, laughing, eating, arguing, gambling on the lives of the little mortals far below. But around the throne itself stood the King's attendants, their thoughts only to please their master. They trembled a little, as dogs tremble on the leash.

In the King's right hand he held, like knife and fork in readiness for a meal, a bolt of thunder and a flash of lightning, and in his other hand a little statuette of Victoria. It was said that he loved Victoria best of all his attendants, because she never questioned his commands and always obeyed instantly, granting victory to navy or army or beleaguered city, meting out triumph or defeat impartially to Greek, to Syrian, to Sudanese or Barbarian. Even now she was away granting victory to the Trojans – or was it the Greeks? On a rocky promontory stood hundred-tongued Fama, holding a trumpet, sounding long, harsh blasts of clarion music to rattle the dreams of sleeping mortals. She too obeyed the King's bidding to the letter, proclaiming his words to Man … whether or not they were true.

With a click of his fingers, the King of the Gods summoned wine. The lesser gods rolled over and held up their empty cups in readiness for the exquisite nectar. The goddess Hebe came at once, running to fulfil her duty as Cupbearer to the Gods. But just as she reached the throne, she caught her foot in the hem of her dress, and pitched forwards almost landing in the King's lap. His nectar she emptied full in his face, so that his curling beard dripped syrupy gold. Thunderbolt and lightning clattered to the floor of Heaven; Victoria's statuette fell and chipped its nose.

The King rose spluttering to his feet and pointed a finger. If she had not been immortal, Hebe would have died then and there. "Never! Never again!" bellowed the King. "Never serve me nectar again! You are not worthy to call yourself Cupbearer to the Gods!"

Hebe curtseyed and ran, knowing better than to make excuses or beg forgiveness. But the gods were left with a problem. For who would bring them their nectar now? Fortuna was too careless and would spill it about like paint. Victoria was always away, roaming the Earth. Fama offered to do it, but her hundred tongues made her too ugly.

So the King took on the shape of an eagle and flapped away to seek a new candidate.

Soaring high over the earth, the eagle has perfect vision. He sees more than any mortal or god. So before long the King of the Olympians glimpsed Ganymede: Prince Ganymede.

At the sight of him the eagle staggered in his flight and tumbled, a ruffle of disordered feathers, through a thousand fathoms of air. Then he regained his balance and swooped low over Mount Ida where the boy stood watching the sun go down.

He was undoubtedly the most beautiful youth ever to have lived. In times gone by, in times to come, there could never be a face so handsome, a bearing so princely. Then and there, the King of the Gods resolved to have Ganymede for his cupbearer, so that each day he might look at this boy and take delight in his beauty.

When Ganymede did not come home that night, his father sent a search party looking for him. But they found only a pair of horses grazing on the peak of Mount Ida — two divine horses, faster and finer than the shaggy nags of Earth. Poor exchange for a son, perhaps, but there was no

reclaiming Ganymede. Even now the eagle was carrying him, on dizzying spirals of warm wind, up to the eyrie peaks of Heaven.

Smothered in feathers, gripped by curving talons, Ganymede found himself breathing air so thin that he panted for breath. Back through the rhythmic beat of wings came a voice large as thunder: "Your duty, boy, shall be to fill the cups of the gods, and for this shall you live on the slopes of Olympus with all the gods of Heaven. For this shall your likeness be hung up in stars. For this shall the city that bore you be blessed … What is your city, boy?"

"I am Ganymede, son of Tros, King of Troy!"

"Then let Troy prosper! Let her name be famous throughout the world. For a time."

"For a time?" said Ganymede as he was set down beside a vast golden throne among flowers whose colours he had never seen before.

"For a time. Nothing lasts for ever, boy," the King reminded him. "Nothing but Heaven and the gods and Ganymede."

CHAINS OF LOVE

VULCAN TAMES HIS WIFE VENUS

*V*enus came in on the roll of a wave — on a chariot of blue water, canopied by the following wave as it curled over her head. She was sea spray; she was flesh-pale as sea spray. In the breaking of the wave she became alive, and as the wave withdrew it left Venus standing naked on the beach. Born where sea and sky kiss, Venus was all Love.

The moment the gods saw her, they began to woo her — Mars and Mercury, Apollo and Neptune. So the King of the Gods, to save a feud in Heaven, declared that Venus must marry at once. She would marry Vulcan, he said.

Poor, deformed Vulcan, Blacksmith of the Gods, was lame and ugly and soot-stained from the fires of his forges. But when he heard the news, his heart beat louder and faster than his own blacksmith's hammer.

"*Marry Vulcan?* Never! I would sooner live single than marry that lump of ugliness!" declared Venus.

But there was no defying the will of the king. The sight of exquisite Venus alongside her dwarfish bridegroom made the gods rock with laughter. Vulcan

13

felt that laughter like sparks from his anvil: it burned him to the quick. Worse still was the look of disgust in his bride's eyes, for he adored her and knew he would never have his love returned.

Sure enough, as soon as Vulcan's back was turned, Venus broke all her wedding vows. She went in search of Mars – handsome, surly god of war, and to him she gave all the kisses she would not give her ugly husband.

Apollo saw the two together as he drove his chariot sun across the linseed blue sky. Partly out of jealousy, partly out of spite, he drove directly to the blacksmith's forge and told him: "Your wife is with Mars, Vulcan. Obviously she prefers his company to yours."

Vulcan's hammer crashed down and his anvil cracked from end to end. Hastily Apollo withdrew, sniggering at the sound of Vulcan's tears hissing on to the forge.

Now, Vulcan was a craftsman – an artist, a genius. Though his head was ugly, the brain inside it was ingenious. He set about forging a net made of steel chains so fine that they were all but invisible, so strong they could snare and hold a fleet of crocodiles. This net he strung up in the branches of a tree, stretching it out like a spider's web over the place where Venus and Mars liked to sit. Then he sat in the tree and waited.

As the lovers met and kissed and whispered together, Vulcan let the net drop. Mars and Venus lay tangled like two chickens in a string bag, and no amount of struggling or cursing or magic could free them. They looked so absurd and shouted so loudly, that the gods came running down from Olympus to stare and to laugh.

Vulcan was content. The gods showed a new respect for him. He did not ask the King to punish his wife: he loved her with the whole great furnace of his heart. The other gods marvelled at such a forgiving nature … but ungrateful Venus only tossed her head, still haughty, still contemptuous.

"What punishment could be worse than to be married to the ugliest man in Heaven?" she said, driving another shard of pain through Vulcan's broken heart.

Perhaps her father heard her and thought she needed to be taught a lesson. Or perhaps it was simply Fate. But Venus soon regretted her words. For she found herself head over heels in love, and not with any handsome god, not with any cupbearer or woodland spirit – not even with her ugly husband. No, Venus fell in love with a *mortal man*.

Anchises of Troy seemed to her more beautiful than golden-haired Apollo or surly, muscular Mars. She wept and bewailed her foolishness – a goddess in love with a mortal! – but could no more break free than if chains of steel bound her to Anchises.

"Swear you will never tell anyone about us – not anyone!" she begged him. "Swear to me you will never boast that you conquered the goddess of love. Swear to me, my love, oh my love!"

Anchises swore, but it was a hard promise to keep – especially when Venus bore him a son – Aeneas. "May I not even tell the boy his mother's name?" he pleaded.

"Never! Never! Or by this hand, it will be the last word you speak. I swear, Anchises, if you ever break your promise, you will die in the instant!" Even as she said it, Venus wished it unsaid, for now she would be afraid every moment, in case Anchises broke his word and died and she had to live everlastingly without him.

Anchises was not a proud or boastful man, but a hundred times a day he was tempted to break his promise. When his son asked, "Who is my mother? Why is she not here in the house, baking bread like all the other mothers? Did she die? Why do you never speak of her? What was her name, at least?"

Finally Aeneas learned that no amount of asking would ever gain him an answer. It seemed to matter less as he grew older. Venus watched over

her son secretly, from the slopes of Heaven and sent him a mortal wife and a son of his own to love.

But even she was powerless to prevent what happened next.

Mars brought war to the city of Troy.

Over the seas came the Greeks, and laid siege to the City of Horses. They fired their arrows into the streets; they challenged the young men of Troy to fight in mortal combat on the shores of the sea.

"Forbid this, Father! Call Mars off! Stop the war!" cried Venus, kneeling before the King of the Gods.

"I commanded it," answered the King. "The people of Earth have grown noisy and troublesome. Ten years of war will thin them out like seedlings and leave only the strongest alive." He held out his cup for nectar. A drop spilled on his finger. "Ganymede? Do you tremble, boy?"

"But my city – Troy! Will Troy be victorious?" asked the Cupbearer to the Gods.

The King strummed his lips; he had not thought so far ahead. "Let us say that if Troy falls, its spirit will live on – somehow, somewhere. This much I will grant you, little Trojan." And he laid a soothing hand on Ganymede's curly hair.

Venus could say no more without admitting her shameful secret. She tried to put out of her mind mortal Anchises and Aeneas besieged within the beautiful walls of Troy. And yet the bonds of love were stronger than even Vulcan could forge, and the prophecies spoke of Troy in flames, of Troy falling, of Troy destroyed ...

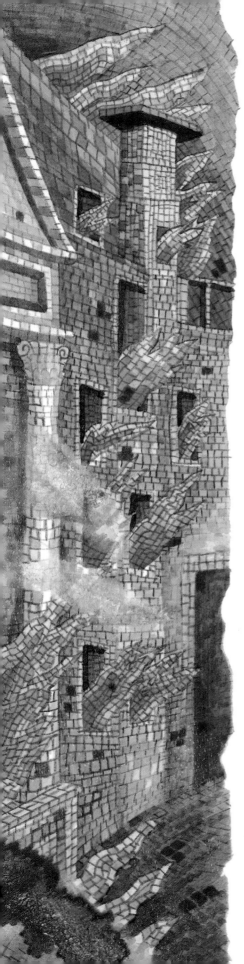

DREAMS OF DESTINY

AENEAS SETS OUT TO FOUND AN EMPIRE

*A*eneas dreamed that a woman's voice was telling him to wake up, and he woke to the sound of buildings falling. There was fire too – a throaty roar like a wild beast eating up Troy. Aeneas knew instantly that the Greeks were inside the city. After ten years of fruitless siege, they had finally found a way in.

Opening the door on to the night, he found the streets bright as day with fire, Greek warriors meting out death to every Trojan man, woman and child. He had to get his family away! Running through the smoke-filled rooms, he caught his young son Iulus by the hand, heaved his old father on to his back, and ran for the harbour, shouting for his household and servants to follow. Not until he reached the waterfront did he realise that his wife was missing, and start back to find her.

He glimpsed her, too, paler than pale, waving to him from an upper window, beyond a curtain of fire. "I am dead, Aeneas!" called her lovely ghost. "Another bride is waiting for you – I will send her to wait for you – on the river bank … !"

Then she was gone. A tower crashed to the ground. The whole city of Troy shivered and sobbed, and the doors of burning buildings slammed like a dozen drumbeats, out of time. Snatching up a burning baulk of timber, Aeneas carried it back to the ship – a piece of Troy, a piece of Troy burning. It seemed important.

Standing at the mast of his ship, his servants grunting and straining at the oars, Aeneas peered astern through the pall of smoke. It seemed to him that figures larger than mere men were beating down the high, white walls of Troy: giant men and women cloaked in light were crazing the palisades with mallets of gold, leaning their shoulders against her towers, breathing fire over the city of his birth.

"What do you see, son?" asked his father, eyes too old for visions.

"The gods themselves," breathed Aeneas, "siding with the Greeks to destroy us!"

Anchises nodded his grizzled head. "Yes, yes. Your mother always said it was Troy's destiny to fall."

"My mother?"

But Anchises would say no more. He never had told, nor ever could tell Aeneas the identity of his mother. Had he not sworn on his life to keep it secret?

Aeneas got away; his destiny demanded it. He sailed to Crete, thinking it was as good a home as any, for a man made homeless. But once landed and asleep on the shores of Crete, he dreamed the most extraordinary dream of his life.

He dreamed that he stood in his house once more, surrounded by the statues of his household gods. "Seek out the land of Italy, Aeneas," their stone mouths seemed to be saying. "There you shall found an empire greater even than Greece or Troy, its feet standing in Africa, its hands reaching into the lands of snow. The great, straight highways of the world shall be its arteries! One day, a city greater than Troy shall sit on seven

hills, and the smoke from its altars rise up to Heaven. Such is the will of the gods!"

Aeneas woke, and lay awake till morning, watching the sparks from the burning Trojan brands spiral upwards towards the stars. Then, at first light, he told his family and servants to reboard the ship.

Again he asked Anchises, "Who was my mother? Did she die when I was born? Why don't I remember her? Why have I never seen her? Why won't you tell me ... ?" But the old man only put a finger to his lips. As Aeneas carried his father aboard, Anchises hung like a sick sheep around a shepherd's shoulders. Every day he was growing weaker.

Wading home from Troy, the gods brushed the ashes and stone dust from their robes and watched the little ships coming and going over the surface of the sea like the pieces of a board game.

"I see a Trojan left alive!" said Juno. "Does he think he can escape the
fate ordained for Troy and all its princes?" And she went to the Keeper of
the Winds and borrowed his leather sack. Loosing its cords, she freed them
all: the north and south, the east and west winds to roll up the ocean and
shake it like a rug.

Aeneas's ship was beaten by blue clods of water large as hills. Shoals
of fish, a debris of dolphins and octopuses and turtles rained down on the
rowers, while wrecks from the sea bed came spinning by. Iulus clung to
his father in terror.

"Hush, child, hush," said Aeneas. "I was born to die a dry death."
Even so, the sea was pouring in over the stern, filling the hull, driving
the whole vessel under …

Just then, Neptune, god of the sea, woken by the huge upheaval in his

bed, thrust his bleary head out of the water to find waterspouts gumming together sea and sky, and everywhere whirlpools dimpling the sea. *"Cease! Be still! Who has been meddling in my domain?"* Then he smoothed flat the sea with his great green hands.

Seeing Aeneas's ship foundering, he raised it to the surface once again, the water gushing out of its bilges, the little Trojan flame still glimmering at its masthead. *"While the seas are mine, only I shall sink ships!"* the god declared, catching the winds like flies between his palms.

The storm had driven them so far off course that they had no idea where they were. But, sighting land, Aeneas and his crew pulled for the shore, where they offered up thanks to the gods for sparing them. Old Anchises, though, was chilled to the bone. Though the light of the campfire glimmered in his eyes, it had no power to warm him.

"Live a little longer, Father!" begged Aeneas. "If the gods are willing, you and I will reach Italy and begin a new life!"

Anchises only smiled sadly. "Your mother will stay by you. She will see you safely to your destiny. My time is over."

"My mother? What do you mean?" said Aeneas.

Anchises shut his eyes. "I don't doubt she loves you as much as I do ... Is she not Love itself, after all? Venus. The goddess Venus." And having broken his promise, Anchises breathed out his last breath, and died, leaving his son, weeping and amazed, on the shores of Libya, beneath the walls of Carthage.

TO HELL AND BACK

AENEAS IN THE UNDERWORLD

*T*he son of Venus! The son of the goddess of love! Little wonder, then, that Aeneas fell in love with Queen Dido the moment they met. Ruler of the sumptuous city of Carthage, Dido was as beautiful as the snowy Atlas peaks. One sight of her, and Aeneas forgot his grief, forgot his dreams, forgot where he was going.

"O mother Venus!" prayed Aeneas, "if ever you cared for this mortal heart of mine, grant me the love of this Queen!"

On the slopes of Olympus Venus sighed a sentimental sigh. How could she refuse her own dear son? Clapping her hands, she summoned her other, immortal son, the boy Cupid. "Go there, dear child, and aim true. No mistakes now! This concerns my son's happiness. So aim your arrows straight and true."

Cupid did better. Speeding down to earth, he nestled close to Dido (who was fond of children, and mistook him for an ordinary boy). Taking one of his arrows in his chubby little fist, he anointed it with the venom called Love … and drove it deep into Dido's heart.

24

As deep as the worst of arrow wounds, Love invaded the Queen of Carthage. She lost all interest in affairs of state. Aeneas lost all thought of journeying further. His household servants, kicking their heels unhappily about the spacious courts and gardens of Carthage, asked each other, "When are we going to set sail? When will he tear himself away?" And Jupiter, watching from Olympus, drummed his fingers impatiently on the parapets of Heaven: *"Does he not know he is keeping history waiting?"* and sent his messenger Mercury down to Carthage. Mercury, on his winged heels, went scudding downwards, carefully carrying a clutch of dreams, which he broke over Aeneas's pillow.

"You have forgotten!"

"No time to waste!"

"The unborn are waiting for you!"

"Ask the Sibyl!"

"Ask the way!"

The dreams harangued Aeneas until he woke with his hands over his ears, heart pounding. Yes, he had abandoned his mission for the sake of his own selfish happiness! Aeneas leapt out of bed. There was no time to lose. Love was sweet, but what of Duty? What of Destiny? His heart yearned after Dido like a little boat tugging at its anchor chain, but he tore himself free and set sail. Queen Dido woke in time to see the mast, with its smoking Trojan brand, dip below the horizon.

She had no 'Duty' to solace her. She had no dreams, no gods whispering in her ear. She had made Aeneas her god and worshipped him day and night. Now he was gone.

"Gather up every shirt he wore, every sheet he ever slept on," she told her servants, "every plate he ate off, every chariot he ever drove!" Her face was a mask of hatred. Dido had all Aeneas's possessions piled up in a bonfire and set alight. Her face was a picture of fury.

'Now she will forget him,' thought her suitors and courtiers. 'Now she will spit on his memory and forget false, lying Aeneas – and good riddance!'

"He abandoned you."

"He jilted you."

"He deceived you," they agreed, smugly sympathising with their Queen.

"He is gone," she said, and the look of hatred melted, gave way to grief. She could pretend no longer to hate Aeneas.

Leaping into the bonfire, she drew a dagger and plunged it into her own breast. It entered through the very wound Cupid's arrow had made, and she died within the space of a single word: *"Aeneas!"*

The Sibyl of Cumae knew much about the future of the world. All day she sat in her cave, on the edge of a vast, trackless forest, writing down prophecies, page after page, volume after volume. Already she knew how Aeneas would avoid the whirlpool Charybdis, the Clashing Rocks, the monsters of the deep sea. But she was also wise enough to see what stood in front of her: an unhappy man, listless and dull-eyed, wishing he were back in Carthage.

"The man who plucks the golden bough
Is he alone the gods allow
To go where no soul else draws breath:
To trespass in the Realm of Death."

That shook Aeneas out of his melancholy. "Hades, you mean? The Underworld? I don't want to go to Hades! Soon enough when I'm dead! Visit the spirits, you mean? How? Why?" He was appalled. "I won't do it!" But he was also intrigued. "How do I find this golden branch? One branch in a forest of this size?"

At that very moment, a small white dove fluttered into the Sibyl's cave and settled on Aeneas's shoulder. Its wing brushed his ear; it pressed its plump breast against his cheek and crooned to him. Then it flew off between the trees. And in that disguise, Venus led her son through the dark, primeval woods which smother the Cumaean countryside.

At the end of the thousandth path, in the darkest heart of the sunless wood, a giant ball of mistletoe glowed like a setting sun. It had no root, as the trees around it had roots, but clung to an oak, drawing its nourishment from the tree as a bat sucks blood.

Climbing up to pick it, climbing down armed with this golden bough, Aeneas ran back to his ship. He set course for Ocean River which flows over the edge of the world. His voyage was lit by twin brands: the Trojan flame and the golden mistletoe.

The darkness grew so dense, so solid that his ship ran aground on it, and he had to continue on foot. Through the Cave of Sleep and Death he passed, where the two giants, Mors and Somnus slept, their poppy crowns askew. In the corners of the room, invisible but for the whites of their rolling eyes, lurked nightmares. A feathery rustling overhead told of sweeter dreams roosting in the eaves. Now and then, a dream or nightmare would dash out through one of two doors – one of ivory, the other of stone: dreams that would come true; dreams to trick and mislead the dreamer. The air of the cave was darkly peppered with seeds from the poppies, and it was all Aeneas could do to stifle his yawns and keep his lids from closing.

The giant Mors slept deepest of all, of course, for his was the sleep of Death.

Beyond the Cave of Sleep lay the River Lethe and its solitary ferryboat, the glaring ferryman demanding his fare from spirits newly arrived. At the sight of Aeneas and the golden bough, however, they fell back, like wolves from a burning brand. Aeneas rode the ferry across Lethe, and the guard dog, three-headed Cerberus tamely let him pass into the Underworld, gazing moon-eyed with all its snarling heads.

That is how Aeneas came to meet with his dead wife once more; with old friends whose adventures had carried them over the brink; with his old father Anchises.

"I have been waiting for you, my son," Anchises said, no longer old, yet not young either; his face empty of either smiles or sorrow. He led Aeneas down clammy tunnels to the door of a cavern quite unlike the rest. "This is the Hall of Unborn Souls," he said, spreading wide his arms. "For fear you turn back, let me show you the people who are relying on you to succeed in your adventure."

The whole cavern shimmered with light from a thousand standing pools. In every pool, shining bright as goldfish, swam restless shreds of life.

"Look. Here are Romulus and Remus; brave Camillus; the world-conquering Caesars. There is Portia, Horatius Cocles, Philemon and Baucis the priests, see? And there! Marcus Curtius. Look! The mighty Augustus — and Virgil the poet, there! Coriolanus the General and Tarquin the Proud." Anchises gave a small shiver. "Some good, some bad, some the stuff of legend. Will you leave them here, in this everlasting dark of Unbeing? Unborn? Nameless? No more than dreams in the mind of the gods?"

"No! Never!" cried Aeneas. Gathering his cloak around him, he asked a blessing from his father's ghost, shouted a farewell to the million watching ghosts, begged forgiveness from Jupiter for wasting so much time, and help from winged Mercury to speed him on his way. Then he left Hades as fast as any galloping nightmare, and returned to his ship more afire than even the golden bough in his hand. "Onwards, men! To Italy! Row for the mouth of the Tiber! There is work to be done!"

Sailing up the Tiber from the sea, Aeneas found green banks where wild grapes grew, forests noisy with boar, glades ghostly with pale deer. Urging his oarsmen higher and higher upstream, he saw at last a red-haired girl sitting on the bank, who lifted her head and watched the ship with curious eyes. Though she had come there to fish, she had the air of someone waiting. The words of his ghostly wife echoed softly through his brain: *"Another bride is waiting for you — I will send her to wait for you — on the river bank ...!"*

"What place is this?" called Aeneas, but she did not understand him. A different language. Another race. Finally, by signs and gestures, they made her understand, and she called back: *"Latium. Ecce Latium."*

Since this was to be his home, the first thing Aeneas had to do was build an altar to Vesta, goddess of hearth and home. The one he raised that evening was no more than a crude pile of stones, but it would have to do. The temple could follow later. Piling the cairn with flowers and branches, Aeneas set them burning with the torch he had carried out of Troy. "Let this flame never go out!" he told his companions. "Let it be tended night and day, for this is the flame of the Past which will light our way to the Future."

On the shrine to Vesta, the golden spray of mistletoe burned with a lively, popping crackle and a bitter-sweet smell.

ROMULUS AND REMUS

TWIN BOYS WHO FOUNDED ROME

*E*mpires rise and fall. The gods, who can see the future, know these things. That is why the gods of Greece gradually shifted ground to the skies over Italy. They came to be known by different names: not Zeus but Jupiter; not Hera but Juno; not winged Hermes but winged Mercury.

Around the shrine to Vesta a great temple was built, its 'vestal' priestesses the unmarried daughters of good families. Because all their love was promised to the goddess, they were forbidden, on pain of death, to give any love to a man.

Rhea Silvia did not: mortal men she could easily have resisted. But the god Mars – quarrelsome Mars, warrior-wild and handsome as only an immortal can be – wooed Rhea Silvia like war besieging a town. He blasted her with love, bombarded her with tender words, shot her full of passion. She could no more resist him than the flowers on the altar could resist the flames which ate them.

Finding she was pregnant, she tried to hide her secret, but soon her slim figure grew as round as a sail,

32

and the other priestesses whispered behind their hands, "What is to be done? Rhea Silvia has broken her vows! Rhea Silvia is giving birth … to twins! Rhea Silvia must die!"

Her mother and father were important citizens – descendants of Aeneas himself. They might have pleaded for the life of their daughter or spirited her away to safety. Instead they upended their hearts and emptied out every last drop of love they had ever felt for her. "Bury her alive, as the law demands," they said. "Rhea Silvia must die."

"But the babies? The twin boys! What will become of them?"

"Throw them into the River Tiber! The pity is that they were ever born!"

Brick by brick, Rhea Silvia was sealed up in her tomb, those last bricks shutting out the sounds and sunlight of the living world. Mars could have shattered her prison with a single breath, but he had long since left Latium to batter some other lady's heart or to raise up war in the world.

As for the twin boys – Romulus and Remus – they were carried naked in a basket to the banks of the Tiber. The servants sent to carry out the task would have tipped them in, midstream. But the Tiber was in flood and the waters milled by with such terrifying force that they set the basket down on the muddy shore and watched till the swollen river swirled the children away towards a watery death.

Ah, but weren't Romulus and Remus the sons of Mars, the descendants of Aeneas? Though their tiny pink fists and feet were powerless to save them, they were strong, healthy boys. The cold did not kill them, nor the river spill them, nor pike snatch them down to a muddy death. The basket was swept helter-skelter downstream until it snagged on tree roots and spun into a backwater where the wild creatures came to drink. A face loomed over the crying boys – a mask with yellow eyes and a mouth full of ravenous teeth. The wolf opened wide her grinny jaws, seized on first Romulus, then Remus, and ran with them to her lair. There she dropped them among the soft, tumbling fur of her hungry cubs …

And there she suckled them, letting them drink, as her cubs drank, from her soft, warm underbelly. A woodpecker perched on a branch nearby to keep watch for danger. (If this seems strange past belief, you should know that wolf and woodpecker are creatures sacred to Mars.)

A herdsman found them. Out one day hunting the wolves who threatened his livestock, he found two big, squalling baby boys, pink and brawling in a wolf-den, and took them home. Now the herdsman was no fool: he knew full well who they were — knew that the law had demanded their death. But he and his wife had no children of their own, and neither civic duty nor fear of punishment counted for anything alongside the joy those children brought them.

Perhaps Romulus and Remus drank down the ferocious courage of the she-wolf as they drank her milk. Perhaps they learned courage and endurance from her as she came and went, feeding and fighting for her young. Or perhaps, as sons of Mars, there was already warrior blood in their veins. But Romulus and Remus grew up into brave, quarrelsome boys who never shunned a fight and who never lost one either.

No shepherd life for them! No life in peaceful Latium. Even before their father told them the story of their birth, they were roaring boys, with roaring friends, their sights pinned on glory. They set their hearts on building a new city, a grand city, a city to rival Troy or Carthage or Athens.

"It shall be called Reme," said Remus.

"Rome, you mean," Romulus corrected him. They quarrelled about it, naturally; it was their way to squabble and row. Brothers do.

But where was their magnificent city to be built?

"Here," said Romulus, "where the she-wolf suckled us!"

"That's not where she suckled us," said Remus with a scornful snort. "It was over there, near that clump of trees."

"Never!" They squabbled and rowed. Brothers do. The gods looked on with mild amusement.

"Let the gods decide!" said Romulus.

"Yes, we'll watch for a sign," agreed Remus. The gods, too, nodded in agreement, and Jupiter sent a flock of ravens to mark the spot fixed by Destiny for the building of the sacred city.

"There! There! Look, three ravens!" cried Remus. "The sacred birds of Jupiter!"

An acorn dropped from the claw of one bird and fell to earth. The brothers, however, were too busy arguing to notice where it fell.

"Seven ravens. There were seven not three," said Romulus.

"What does it matter? I saw them first. So I choose where Reme is built."

"But I saw more ravens than you!" protested Romulus. "So I shall build in my chosen place. You can do as you like … and it will be Rome, not Reme!" They exchanged a string of insults. Brothers do. The gods frowned a little at their squabbling. Time was going to waste.

36

Obstinate Romulus began to build – where the Tiber snaked between seven hills, where the sunbeams were blade-sharp and golden, and where the stones were mossy massive – heaping the boulders into a wall.

"Call that a wall?" jeered Remus. "I've seen bigger pigsties!" and he jumped over the low walling, his feet dislodging pebbles, his taunts loud and sneering. To and fro he jumped, deriding Romulus's work until all brotherly affection dissolved in Romulus and he hated his brother with a hot loathing. Brothers can. He picked up a boulder. "You do that once more …"

Remus jumped the wall. A whole section slumped down in a landslide of rocks and pebbles. Romulus lifted the boulder and brought it down on his brother's head. Remus was dead before he even hit the ground. "Thus die all those who ever try to leap the walls of Rome!" Romulus crowed, as his young warrior friends ran to the spot and crowded round.

Then Romulus wept, because he had killed his best friend in the world, and all for the sake of a pile of stones.

The gods looked on with distaste. How could the destiny of an empire rest on the shoulders of such men?

"It is good," said Mars, dry-eyed, stony-faced. "It is good that blood should water the foundations of Rome."

But Jupiter shook his head. "They were fools to quarrel," he said.

"Their foolishness does not stop there," said Venus softly. "Look at them. An army of men building a city for themselves. How can there be a city without women? Where do they hope to find sons and daughters – floating on the Tiber or crying among the wolves?"

STOLEN WIVES

THE THEFT OF THE SABINE WOMEN

*I*t was not long before the men of Rome noticed the lack of women. Though the city was finished (and it was very fine), there was no one in it to bake them bread or wash their shirts, nobody to tell them they were brave or handsome or wonderful.

"I have the answer," said Romulus. "Are we not warriors? Do we not have the cunning of Aeneas and the strength of Mars? We shall take wives enough for every house in Rome!"

He invited the neighbouring tribe to visit the gleaming new city of Rome – to join in celebrations at its completion.

The Sabines were handsome people, their womenfolk tall and red-haired and beautiful. Once the visitors were sat down to dine, their weapons stacked by the door, their reflexes slow from drinking, the Romans swept in like a whirlwind and snatched the women up by the hair, by the wrists, by the waist, carrying them off to the safety of locked rooms. The men and boys were driven out of the city like leaves in front of a broom, and before they could gather their wits, found themselves sitting outside the gates, robbed of their daughters, sisters and wives.

No tears, no pleas, no prayers, no offers of ransom or threats of revenge – "Our men will never rest till they have us back!" – softened the hearts of the Roman men. They were too busy choosing themselves wives.

"That one in the grey."

"The fat one for me!"

"The one with the green eyes."

They were like children at a pet shop choosing rabbits or kittens.

Married against their will, the Sabine women found themselves keeping house, singing songs, tending wounds, baking bread and warming the beds of Roman husbands. They swore never to forgive their captors, to hate them for ever.

But of course hatred is as hard to keep alight as a hearth fire. The Roman men were not monsters; in most respects, they were just like Sabine men. Some were handsome, some funny, some athletic, some artistic. Some liked to dip their olive bread in their wine; some were afraid of spiders. Not a day passed but the Sabine wives remembered their Sabine homes and husbands and the children lost to them. And yet this new life had its merits.

Babies were born – babies with Roman noses and Sabine hair – and their fathers doted on them and carved them little wooden boats to float on the Tiber. Romans made good fathers and honourable husbands. Now and then, their Sabine wives had to admit as much.

Then one day the Sabines came back.

Of course they came. Did Romulus really suppose that they could live without women any more than the Romans could? Did he really suppose the Sabines would rest until they had recaptured their wives, their mothers, their daughters?

From Rome's high walls, the Sabine army was sighted by the lookouts. The great doors of the temple of Janus (which stand open in times of war) swung ajar like a mouth gaping, and the men scrambled to arm themselves for battle.

"Never fear, wives!" yelled the Sabine warriors from outside the walls. "We have come to rescue you, and we shall not rest till every Roman lies awash in his own blood!"

"Never fear," said the Romans to their wives as they whetted the swords and took up their battle shields. "We shall be victorious by sunset!"

The women did not reply except to pull their scarves over their faces and rock silently to and fro. They drifted together into the forum — women torn in two by divided loyalties. At last, lifting up their small fry, cradling their babies, they broke into a run. Out of the city gates they ran, to where the Roman army was drawn up in battle lines before the massed ranks of the Sabines.

"Stop! Stop! Enough!" they shouted, holding up babies and children

shoulder high. Baby clouts flapped whitely like flags of surrender. "Are we bones that you fight over us like dogs? Stop! Are we to see our husbands slaughtered by our brothers, our sons killed by our own fathers? Stop! Which of you could win a victory without breaking our hearts by it? Which of you could win today without winning our hatred? If women ruled, there would be no war, for women are always the losers in any battle. Well, then! If you must fight, you must cut your way through us first, and through your little children! Better for us to die than that you hack our hearts in pieces!"

The jogging run of both advancing armies slowed to a halt. They glared at one another between the upraised arms of their women. They craved the glory of battle; they loved fighting. But the women stood their ground, the children watching with big, terrified eyes. A silence fell, broken only by the crying of babies.

And the watching gods smiled at the men's predicament. At least Venus smiled and tucked a daisy behind the ear of Mars as the god of war watched helpless, gnashing his teeth with frustration. For the Romans and Sabines were striking a truce – surly and grudging, it's true, but a truce even so. There would be no war. The women had won their way, and for a brief time at least, the doors of the temple of Janus swung closed again to declare a time of peace.

A WILD GOOSE CHASE

THE STORY OF PHILEMON AND BAUCIS

A knock at the door. A pair of passing strangers. Philemon and Baucis did not know the two men on their doorstep, but they had never yet failed to offer a warm welcome to anyone who called at their little cottage.

"Come in! Sit down! My wife will cook you supper!" said Philemon.

His wife tugged at his sleeve. She did not need to say more. Both of them knew there was no food in the house. Not a bite. Baucis and Philemon themselves had been living on eggs and olives for days. There was not even any bread.

Philemon smiled sadly at Baucis and she smiled sadly back. "It's the goose, is it?" he said.

"The goose it is," she replied.

Clio was all they had left. She was more like a pet than a farmyard fowl. And yet guests are a blessing sent by the gods, and guests must be fed. So Philemon fetched his sharp axe, and Baucis began to chase the goose, trying to drive it into the cottage.

Jupiter sat back in his chair and waited patiently for dinner. "Do you think we should help?" he said to Mercury, hearing the commotion in the yard.

"I know we shall have a wait," replied Mercury.

"Here – you try," said Baucis, passing the axe to Philemon.

The goose was squawking, Baucis was yelping, and Philemon was coughing as he ran about wielding the axe. He struck at Clio, but the goose moved, and he demolished a bush. He swung again and hit the wooden pail. The goose shrieked with outrage, then with terror, and slapped about on her big, triangular feet – plat, plat, plat – skidding into their home-made altar piled high with flowers, into the fish-drying rack, into the washing on the tree. Olives rained down on the roof of the shack.

"Do you think we should go?" said Jupiter, as he and Mercury listened to the wild goose chase and their hungry stomachs growled quietly.

At last Philemon and Baucis cornered the goose against the cottage door. Her orange beak gaped. Philemon raised the axe … And Clio bolted backwards into the shack, running round the room like a black-footed pillow-fight until she caught sight of Jupiter.

Now animals are not so easily fooled by disguises, and although Jupiter and Mercury were dressed as peasants, in woollen tunics and straw hats, she instantly recognised the King of the Gods and threw herself on his mercy. Neck outstretched, eyes bulging, she ran straight between his knees and into his lap. He was overrun with goose.

"A thousand pardons, friend," gasped Baucis, crawling in at the door, her hair stuck with goose quills. "Won't you take an olive while you wait?"

Jupiter stroked the goose which stood paddling on his thighs, and spat out a few feathers. "Shield me! Save me! Protect me!" said the goose, in the language of geese.

Jupiter tickled it under the beak. "Your hospitality is a marvel, dear Philemon, gentle Baucis. In all my long travels over the face of the world, I have never met such unselfish hosts. Here is your only goose, and you were ready to cook it for us! Your generosity surpasses that of the gods themselves!"

"Now, sir," said Baucis sternly. "You may be a guest, but I'll have no ill spoken of the gods in this house. Though we have little to offer, the gods have been good to us, have they not, my love?"

"They have, they have," said Philemon. Mercury concealed a grin.

"And they shall be good to you ever after!" declared Jupiter, rising to his feet. He rose and rose, till his head touched the rafters, and his face brightened till the room was light as day. His disguise fell away, and Mercury folded it small and smaller till it fitted inside one fist and was gone.

"As you see, I am Jupiter, King of the Gods, and this is my messenger, Mercury. We like to travel the world and visit the people whose sacrificial smoke perfumes the halls of Heaven. But travel where we may and stay where we might, we never met with such hospitality as yours! Name any favour, and it shall be your reward. A small kingdom, perhaps? A palace? A chest of sea treasure from the vaults of Poseidon? Wings to fly, or the gift of prophecy? Name it!"

Mercury looked uneasy. He had seen the greed and ambition of mortals all too often. This mild-looking couple would probably demand to be gods and to dine at the table of the gods; would ask for immortality or a banner of stars wide as the Milky Way, spelling out 'Philemon the Philanthropist', 'Baucis the Beautiful'.

Baucis looked at Philemon, and Philemon smiled back and wrung his hat shyly between his hands. "Almighty Jupiter, you have done our little house such an honour today that we have hardly breath enough to speak our thanks. Our greatest joy in life has always been to worship at our humble little altar – out there in the yard. What more could we ask than to go on doing that – oh, and both to die at the same hour, so that we may never be parted. My Baucis and I."

Jupiter complained of a speck of dust in his eye and went outside. He could be heard blowing his nose loudly. When he ducked back through the door, his eyes were quite red-rimmed. "Come, priest and priestess of my shrine! Your temple awaits you!"

All of a sudden, the draughty, ramshackle little hut disintegrated, like a raft of leaves on a river. Around and above it rose the pillars of a mighty temple. The simple cairn of stones which had served for an altar still stood there, piled with firewood and swagged with flowers, but now it stood on a marble floor, and from that floor rose forty marble pillars cloaked with beaten gold, supporting a roof gilded with stars. The living quarters for priest and priestess were piled with feather mattresses and silken pillows, and priestly robes of soft cotton hung waiting about the shoulders of Carrara statues.

Already, from all corners of the landscape, pilgrims were setting out at a run to visit the marvellous new temple of Jupiter, whose red roof signalled to them across miles of open countryside. Philemon and Baucis would be kept busy receiving their sacrifices, tending the sacrificial flame, sweeping up the ashes …

But they thrived on the hard work, just as they had always done. The worshippers brought not only flowers for the altar but baskets of delicious food for the priest and priestess whose fame spread far and wide. Tirelessly they worked until, being mortal, even Baucis and Philemon became exhausted. Watching from the terraces of Heaven, Jupiter saw them pause now, each time they passed one another, and lean one against the other for a moment's rest, Baucis laying her head on Philemon's shoulder.

"They are weary," said Mercury.

"You are right," said Jupiter. "It is time for them to rest."

So instead of breathing in the fragrance from the altar below, he breathed out – a breath which wafted away the white robes of priest and priestess and left behind two noble trees at the very door of the temple. One was an oak, the other a linden tree, and they leaned one towards another, their branches intertwined, casting welcome shade over the threshold.

Clio the goose liked to rest there at noon, preening her breast feathers and singing like a jackass.

LIBER-ALITY

HOW ROME RECEIVED ITS MOST PRIZED BLESSING

*F*alernus was a poor man, but rich in friends. His door was never shut to those who needed a word of advice, a shoulder to cry on, the loan of a fishing rod, a bite to eat. Above all, Falernus was a hospitable man, so that when Liber, god of the countryside, passed by one hot and dusty day, he received a kingly welcome from Falernus without even giving his name.

"Fish, sir, from the river! Cheese from my own cow! Here's bread, sir, such as I have, and olives from my tree. Rest yourself, do: noon is no time for anyone to be travelling. I'll fetch you a cup of water from the spring."

"Water?" said Liber, wincing with disgust. "I am accustomed to drinking wine."

Falernus's face fell. "You shame me, then, sir. For I have none to give you – not a drop. I would run to my neighbours, but I'd only share my shame with them. There's been no wine drunk in these parts for many a year."

"At banquets in the city I see it," said the god moodily.

"Ah yes, sir. Anything can be had for money, I suppose, and there's plenty of money in Rome. But when a thing has to be brought by ship over the ocean or by horse and cart along a hundred miles of road, it costs more to buy than our kind can afford."

Liber saw that there were tears in the creases of the sunburned cheeks because Falernus had failed in his hospitality. "I had not meant to slander your fine springwater, friend!" he said hurriedly. "I was simply going to ask if you minded me drinking the wine I carry with me … perhaps you would do me the honour of drinking with me?" And he fetched a jug from the saddle of his donkey and poured two cups of wine from it. What a remarkable jug it must be — or what a remarkable donkey — that it had not slopped and spilled on the journey.

Falernus drank delightedly. He had never tasted anything so delicious as the rich red wine from Liber's jug. Oddly enough, however much he drank, his cup never seemed to be empty. In fact he drank all afternoon and never once did he drain the dregs.

By that time, naturally, he was extremely … sleepy. He and Liber had sung every song they knew, recited every poem, exchanged all jokes they understood and several they did not. The sides of Falernus's shabby hut

spun like the walls of a whirlpool. He was just demonstrating a trick involving three live chickens and a squashed olive when all of a sudden the wine got the better of him and he sank slowly on to the table and fell asleep with his cheek in the cheese. Liber got up, hooked his jug on to his saddle again, and went on his way in the blue coolness of the evening.

When Falernus woke, he had a very hazy memory of the day before. He could remember having a visitor, but not the visitor's name. He could remember having emptied the larder, but not why the chicken smelled of olive oil. He could remember the start of the joke about the elephant in the *frigidarium*, but not the punchline. Come to that, he could remember this bare, wind-leaky, rot-mildewed little hut of his, but not the view from its window.

Why was the garden full of vines? Why did the vines stretch away, in serried rows, over every field and hill as far as his bloodshot eyes could see? Falernus tottered outside and found his neighbours roaming up and down the vines, fingering the big bunches of ripening grapes and gasping with rapturous wonder. "The gods have blessed us, Falernus! The gods have blessed us overnight! What did we ever do to deserve such a blessing?"

And though Falernus had to agree — there was no greater boon that the gods could have granted his village — he could not for the life of him think *why* the Immortals should have leaned so far out of Heaven to plant a million vines on his doorstep.

KISSED BY THE MOON

THE STORY OF DIANA AND ENDYMION

*T*he chariot of the Moon goddess Diana is old now, tarnished by night rains, dented by collisions with owls and flitterbats. See how its silver-white sides are mottled with imperfections. Once, long ago, when her chariot was still gleaming new, Diana used to drive across the night sky with barely a thought for the sleeping world below.

Then one night, happening to glance down at the silvered glory of the Roman countryside, she caught sight of a shepherd sleeping on a Tuscan hilltop. The moonbeams lit his sheep first, whitely luminous, then his woollen tunic, then the shine of his curly hair. His sleeping face was beautiful past any she had seen before.

Sleepy astronomers watching late that night rubbed their eyes in disbelief. For the Moon, contrary to all the laws of Nature, appeared to dip in mid-sky and to rest for a moment on the summit of a Tuscan hill.

Down climbed Diana to study more closely the young shepherd's face. She bent over him, holding her hair for fear it would brush his face. The more she stared, the more she admired what she saw – the fringe of lashes, the tilt of the cheekbones, the downy softness of a jawline never shaved.

She looked … and she loved, and because this sleeping mortal would never know she had done it, she bent and kissed his sleeping lips.

Somewhere in the musty meadows of sleep, a dream galloped down on Endymion – a glorious, silvery dream which filled him with inexpressible happiness. He dreamed a face too beautiful to belong to any mortal woman. He dreamed of silken hair held back by her fingers, a smell of night-scented stocks, a hand resting on his chest. Roused almost to waking, his lids flickered, and he thought he saw a hank of hair fanning out as a woman turned away. By the time he had fully woken, there was no one to be seen – only the Moon gliding overhead towards its setting place among the cedar trees.

Endymion was filled with emotions so odd that he hardly knew whether to laugh or cry. His dream had been so sweet – he could still almost feel the bruise of a kiss upon his mouth – that he wanted to go back to sleep at once, to recapture that elusive bliss. The next night Endymion curled up in his cloak almost as soon as night fell, praying that he might enjoy the same dream again.

And Diana, harnessing the horses to her chariot, fumbled with the buckles, so eager was she to be rising. Would her shepherd be there again tonight, sleeping on his hilltop? Could he really be as exquisitely handsome as she remembered? Trailing diaphanous moonbeams across the Tuscan countryside, Diana leaned over the side of her chariot, scanning the darkened landscape for a glimpse of Endymion. And there he was! Asleep once again on his hilltop, surrounded by lambs. He looked more beautiful than ever.

Somewhere in the birch-silver wood of sleep, Endymion dreamed that same wonderful dream – a woman bending to kiss his mouth, white hands ruffling his hair, a voice whispering, "Sleep on, sleep on, Endymion my love."

Endymion no longer cared about the sunlit hours. He spent them longing for nightfall, for the dream which repeated itself each moonlit

night, filling him with indescribable bliss. He fretted for fear his dreaming would end; no earthly woman interested him as much as the face which haunted his dream.

One night Diana, reining in her chariot, leapt down to steal her nightly kiss. But, as she bent low over Endymion's curly head, she noticed a single grey hair in among the gold ones, a deepening of the creases above his brow. Her shepherd was as beautiful as ever, but that grey hair, that crease – they were proof that Endymion was mortal and would grow older with every passing day. He would worry about the price of wool, the cost of bread. The wind would weather his skin, and age or illness would bring him pain and weariness. Diana could not bear to think of her beloved suffering any such hardships. So, next night, she sewed a hammock of moonbeams and laid Endymion inside it, towing the hammock behind her silver car. She carried him all the way to the western horizon, to Mount Latmos, Land of Forgetfulness. There, in a cave, she laid him on a bed of lambswool, whispering the magic which would prevent him waking – ever.

Now he sleeps out of reach of Time or Unhappiness or Work, in a dreamless oblivion. Only as the Moon's goddess drives her chariot over the rim of the world does he begin to dream. He dreams that a woman drives up to his cave, and there she unharnesses her chariot and looses her horses to graze. Then she comes to him and, circling his head with her arms, she tells him all she has seen on her chariot ride – the dying campfires of sleeping armies, the porpoises leaping over the sea, the wolves prowling around sheepfolds, the lullabies sung by mothers to their babies.

Then she bends to kiss him, and her face is as lovely as the morning star melting into the light of day.

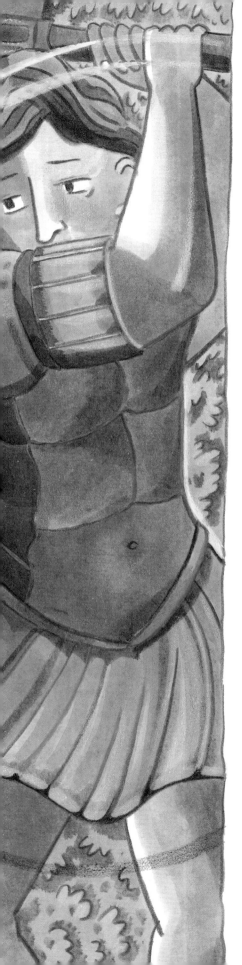

THE MAN WHO CUT DOWN TREES

ERISYCHTHON PAYS A TERRIBLE PRICE

*I*n the days when even the trees worshipped the gods of Rome, their first love was for Ceres, goddess of harvests, guardian of the seasons, bringer of fruitfulness. All the length and breadth of the Roman world, copses and spinneys were held sacred to Ceres: no one was permitted to cut them down.

Erisychthon, though, when he looked at a tree did not see green-robed priestesses, hands upraised in praise, swaying in elegant dance. He saw firewood.

In fact he shouldered his axe and whistled his way to a circle of ancient oaks, and there he began to hack at one so hard that the whole copse shuddered.

"Don't, Erisychthon!" cried passers-by. "Don't cut down the sacred oak! Ceres will be angry!"

"What do I care how the gods feel? A tree is a tree. It's good for nothing but acorns in the summer and firewood in the winter. Now get out of my way and let me work."

Thud, thud, thud: his great axe bit deep into the tree, and red flecks stained his tunic.

58

"The tree is bleeding, Father!" cried his little daughter Melia. "You are murdering the tree!"

"Sap. Nothing but sap," said the woodcutter, who did not believe that trees could bleed. "Are you as stupid as the rest of these superstitious fools?"

The oak tree groaned in agony as the axe cleaved to her innermost ring, to the oldest central timber. The crowd began to jeer and throw clods of earth, trying to make him stop, but Erisychthon only came after them with his axe and chased them away. Then, with a great noise like a ship foundering, the oak tree fell, spilling its green tresses along the ground.

Erisychthon began to chop at the next tree, and the next.

Not until all the trees lay lopped and logged did Ceres happen by and see the crime Erisychthon had committed. She saw the leaves like spilled teardrops; she saw the blood on the grass, and she wondered what manner of man had done this to living, holy trees. "Only an empty man, a heartless man, a hollow man could have done this," she concluded.

"All that work has made me hungry," said Erisychthon as he reached home. He ate all the cheese on the table and all the fruit in the bowl, but still he felt hungry.

So he ate all the olives on the tree outside, all the barley in the hopper, all the milk in the cow. It only seemed to make him hungrier. He ate not only his own supper but his daughter's too, complaining, "Why such small portions? I'm still famished!"

Filling his purse with money, he went to the market and bought whole haunches of venison, whole sides of bacon, whole trestles of smoked fish. But though he ate everything he bought, within the hour he was still ravenous with hunger.

He spent all the money he had – borrowed as much as anyone would lend him – and then began selling his possessions – his cloak, his donkey, his axe. But though he was able to buy all the vegetables in the market, all the fish off the boats, though he dragged home a whole ox to roast and raided his neighbours' orchards at night, Erisychthon could not satisfy the gnawing hunger that rumbled in his stomach.

"Father! Father! There is nothing left to sell!" cried his daughter, watching him cram his mouth with swill from the pig's trough (the pig had been eaten long since). "Pray to the gods to take this terrible hunger of yours away!"

But Erisychthon only looked at her with a glistening eye and said, "I hear a young slave-girl fetches a good price."

Tossing Melia over his shoulder, he carried her, crying and pleading, down to the bay where the slave ships moored. "Wait here till I find someone to buy you," he said indistinctly, chewing on a mouthful of shellfish. When he had gone, Melia raised her face to the sky and her hands to her face. "O you gods, take pity on me! Must I pay for my father's foolishness?"

A wave curled upward out of the sea, a crook of Neptune's sea-blue finger, encircling Melia's feet. Suddenly she was no longer wearing dress

and shawl, but a rough canvas tunic and oiled woollen leggings. The hands against her face were gnarled and rough. When Erisychthon returned with a slave merchant, he saw only a fisherman standing by the shore. "Where's my daughter? Where did she run off to?"

"No one here but me," replied Melia, and her voice emerged deep and gruff. Erisychthon cursed furiously while the slave merchant put the bag of gold back into his pocket.

"No, please! I must have food! I'm starving!" Erisychthon begged.

The man looked him up and down contemptuously, this big, paunchy, red-faced glutton chewing on a live crab.

Alone on the beach once more, Erisychthon wiped his mouth with the back of his hand. He tasted the salty tang of his own sweat. He could not help himself. Instinctively he took a bite. It hurt: he yelped with pain. But

at least his mouth was full. Maddened with hunger, he
raced along the beach, but he had scoured it clean of all
crustaceans, all seaweed, had robbed the gulls of their usual
meal of rubbish scraps, and still he was hungry! Licking the
bite in his hand, he tasted the salty savour of blood and took
another, larger bite, this time out of his fat forearm.

"Come quickly, someone! It's my father! You have to
stop him! He is eating …" Melia caught hold of people as
she ran along the village street. "It is too horrible! You
have to come and stop him!"

They followed her willingly enough: they had no
grudge against Melia, who was a pleasant, devout little
thing. So they ran with her down to the beach. But by
the time they got there, there was nothing to be seen
of her father. You see, Erisychthon had eaten his last meal,
down to the very last crumb – gobbled himself up, arm
by leg by rib by hair, and left nothing for the crabs.

Ceres was revenged on the man who had cut
down her trees.

TELL TALE TIT

THE LOVE STORY OF MERCURY AND LARA

Shrill as a parakeet, loud as a cockerel, Lara chattered all day long. Never mind whether anyone was listening, never mind whether she had anything worth saying, she kept up a steady rickety-racket of chatter that drove the gods to distraction.

"I think the sea would be prettier if it were green," she might say, or "I wish I understood what the camels were saying … Why should socks go in pairs? Wouldn't Tuesday rather come after Saturday?"

"Will she never pause for breath?" groaned the gods. "Will she never wait for an answer? Will she never stop?"

Worst of all, Lara, nymph of the babbling fountains, did not know that some things are never to be said aloud – like Jupiter's little secrets, like snatches of dangerous gossip. "Did you hear what Almighty Jupiter gave his sweetheart yesterday?" prattled Lara to no one in particular. "Oh, you should have heard the sweet names he called her when she was sitting in his lap!"

"Should I, indeed?" hissed Juno, Jupiter's jealous wife. Her lips tightened and she ground her teeth

64

alarmingly. "Then *do* tell." Lara talked for an hour without pausing for breath. She spilled every one of Jupiter's well-kept secrets.

Juno went after her husband like a hornet, calling him names that were neither Roman nor Greek nor at all polite. She hurled things, too — a jug of hippocras, a lyre, a peacock, the boy Cupid … Then she showered him with reproachful tears and slaps and pinches, and swore to turn all his little girlfriends into cows or bears or platypuses.

"Lara will pay for this!" snarled Jupiter, nursing his stinging cheeks. "That meddling chatterbox has prattled her last word of gossip. Where is the gabbling little wretch?"

In his rage, he took hold of the nymph by her long hair and reached his fingers into her mouth, chanting,

> *"Tell tale tit,*
>
> *Your tongue shall be split*
>
> *And all the little birds and beasts*
>
> *Shall have a piece of it!"*

Lara screamed, but no sound came from her throat. Lara apologised for the damage she had done, but no word formed itself in her empty mouth. Lara begged forgiveness, but Jupiter could no longer hear her shrill, irritating voice. For Lara had no voice, no tongue, no means of speaking. "Mercury! Escort this troublemaker down to the Underworld and let her live there for all time, silent as the grave!" With a crash of thunder

and a slamming of heavenly doors, Jupiter was gone, and Lara stood facing Mercury, messenger of the gods, a thread of blood trickling from the corner of her silent mouth.

Her shocked eyes were huge, he noticed, the colour of water. Her deathly white face was as pretty as foaming water. Her long hair fell about her like a cascade of gold, and she trembled from head to foot. Mercury took his prisoner by the hand, and led her off the slopes of Heaven, down and on down towards the realm of Dis.

"Jupiter does not like to be found out," said Mercury, though he realised as he said it that Lara had found that out for herself. "Perhaps he will forgive you in time," he said, though they both knew that would never happen. "Perhaps you would like to rest now," he said. "We have been travelling a great many hours."

Lara sat down at once. She did not argue or complain: how could she? She did not ask questions about the Underworld, or talk of the friends and places lost to her for ever: that would have been impossible. When Mercury talked, she listened without interrupting. When he suggested they continue on their way, she got up at once, without argument. What else could she do?

But Mercury was impressed. Never before had he met such a demure, peaceable companion. Never before had he spent so long in a woman's company without fretting to be gone. Now he came to look at her, Lara really was very pretty. "May I kiss you?" he asked, and Lara, naturally, voiced no objection.

Long before they reached the Underworld, Mercury and Lara were deeply in love. She too had stopped talking for long enough to think about her life – about her faults, about the things she valued, the hopes she harboured, about the sweet possibilities of Love. Instead of delivering his prisoner into the hands of Dis, Lord of the Underworld, Mercury spirited her away to sunlit woods, to a peasant cottage by a little stream, and there he married her.

They had two children, known simply as the Lares, 'Children of Lara'. Somehow it did not matter that Lara could not speak: her happiness was too great for words in any case.

The couple in the cottage in the wood were so prized by their neighbours – "Such a quiet pair …" "Never a cross word …" "And such lovely, soft-spoken children!" – that they had no need of ambrosia to eat or hippocras to drink. There was always a door open to them at mealtimes, always a place for them at some rough trestle table. Mercury was so witty, and Lara was *such* a good listener.

But, fearful that Jupiter's anger might one day reach out of heaven and hurt their beloved children, Mercury made the Lares invisible, and hid them among the people of the world, asking the Mortals to take care of his poor, unfortunate babies.

And the people of Earth (well, any whose roof had ever been scorched by lightning or whose sheep had been scared by thunder or whose vines had turned white with blight) took the little girl and boy to their hearts. In setting their tables, they always laid one extra place, served one extra portion, filled one extra cup, just in case the Children of Lara were there, unseen and so very, very soft-spoken that their little voices could not be heard.

BURNING
THE BOOKS

THE SIBYL AND HER PROPHECIES

*A*ll this while, the Sibyl had sat writing, line after line, scroll after scroll. The future she had foreseen for Aeneas and his children became the present, then passed into history, but by then screeds more had already been written about the days to come. The Sibyl saw the future as a view from a window, and wrote it down in her spidery, tangled hand, so that her prophecies grew like cloth from a loom, like a scarf from knitting needles.

Nine books of prophecies the Cumaean Sibyl wrote, though that view of hers became less and less pleasant. In the end she rolled up her nine scrolls, laid them in a raffia basket, and carried them all the way to Rome.

She found the place very changed from the days when Romulus had ruled there; a big, prosperous sprawling place now, its map as complicated as a page of handwriting. She found it gloomy, too, its alleyways full of weeping, its children hollow-eyed with worry. After six good kings had come a seventh: Tarquin the Proud, a despot and a bully. The Roman virtues of Love and Duty

69

were nowhere in his nature, and he ruled Rome as if it were a dog walking at his heel.

Of course the Sibyl knew all this – had seen it coming long before Tarquin had even been born.

"Hail, Tarquin of Rome. I bring books for you to buy," said the bent old woman, shuffling towards the King.

"Books? What do I want with books?" sneered Tarquin. "I know everything worth knowing already."

"What is written in these books no man knows, for they concern the future," said the old woman. "I am the Sibyl of Cumae. I am weary now with writing. My inkwell is dry. Now I wish to sit and nod in the shade of an olive tree, and think of things past instead of things to come. So pay me one hundred pieces of gold and I will give you these nine books of prophecies, so that you may read what the future holds in store for Rome."

"Who let in this mad old crone?" sniggered Tarquin. "Pay a hundred pieces of gold for some lunatic scribblings? I wouldn't pay one groat to see you eaten by lions. Get out."

From the raffia basket the Sibyl took one scroll and held it out towards one of the lamps which lit the room. As it flared up, she dropped it on the floor of the throne-room. Every eye watched it burn, watched the secrets of the future charring and turning to ash.

"Now there are only eight, Tarquin. Do you always laugh at your elders and betters?"

Tarquin curled his lip in contempt (though there was something disturbing about seeing a scroll burn – all those names, those places, those predictions). "Weather forecasts and gobbledegook," he jeered. "I shall have you put out of doors like a cat."

The Sibyl took a second scroll from her basket and lit it from the embers of the first. It flared up and was gone, ashes scurrying away under the furniture. No one moved to eject the Sibyl: there was not a man there who had not heard of the ancient Sibyl of Cumae and her writings.

"Take care, old witch. You will have nothing left to sell. Already your stock is worth only eighty gold pieces."

"Ah, but the cost has gone up to a thousand," said the Sibyl.

Tarquin grew hot with anger. "What? Pay more for less? What kind of a fool do you think I am? It's eighty or nothing!"

The Sibyl took another scroll and lit it from a guttering candle. The watching crowd gasped and murmured. It was as if the very future itself was going up in flames. Tarquin glimpsed the word 'Rome' as it blackened, smouldered, then burned to ash.

"What kind of fool do you think I am that I will pay a thousand for the ramblings of a mad witch?"

"A fool needs words of wisdom more than a wise man," said the Sibyl. "That is why I came to you. The price is now two thousand."

Tarquin jumped to his feet and lunged about the room. "Do you hear her? Does she insult me as well as bore me with her worthless nonsense?" But the courtiers only stared at the growing heap of ash on the floor — their future, the future of their children, their city, the world, lost to the fire. They were willing Tarquin to pay. When he said, "I won't be held to ransom like this!" they moaned and bit the sides of their hands.

"No!" they groaned as the Sibyl burned another scroll. The room was full of black floating specks now, though Tarquin could not tell them apart from the flecks of anger floating in front of his eyes. She was perfectly right: of course he desperately wanted the scrolls. But then they were his by rights. Everything in Rome was his by rights. "Give me those scrolls!" he raged.

"For three thousand gold pieces I will," said the Sibyl, and burned another scroll.

Tarquin looked around him. He knew they hated him, these toga-ed statesmen and battle-hardened generals. He knew how their fingers itched to draw their daggers against him. He glanced back at the burning vellum and saw his own name written in the Sibyl's scrawl; saw it circled in fire, then burning. He went to stamp out the flames, but the fragile scorched scroll only crumbled to dust under his sandal.

"Very well! Have your extortion money, you old hag!"

The Sibyl reached for another scroll, her puckered old face hardened against his insults.

"All right, I said!" cried Tarquin. "Stop! Please … the books. I beg you. Please. Madam. Lady. Please."

Thus three of the original nine great Sibylline Books were carried for safekeeping to a shrine on Capitol Hill, where the wisest men in Rome

studied them, puzzling over the handwriting like men struggling through a thorn hedge.

Tarquin, when his courage and pride returned, sent to have the Sibyl killed, but she was nowhere to be found.

Whenever a problem arose, the people looked to the Sibylline prophecies for an answer. What should they do? What would they do (for the Future was already decided). How would the thing turn out? And whenever they could not find a solution in those three precious scrolls on Capitol Hill, they blamed Tarquin. He had robbed them of two-thirds of their future. When they thought about it, he had robbed them of two-thirds of their freedom, too: their money, their civic rights, their reputation as the noblest of city-states. Had the time not come to be rid of Tarquin the Proud? They scoured the Sibyl's scrolls for an omen, a portent, for encouragement to rise up and rebel. But Tarquin's promised fate had been burned to ashes. Perhaps that was a portent in itself . . .

So they rose up and rebelled – ousted Tarquin and took back their freedom. As the Sibyl had known all along, men will find in prophecy everything they want to find, whether they have three volumes or nine.

LITTLE OLD BOY

TAGES SHARES HIS GREAT KNOWLEDGE

*W*hen his plough uncovered the first tuft of grey, Tarchon thought: A bird. A dead bird. But when he looked closely, he saw that the wisps had more the texture of hair than of feathers.

He dug with his hands, scooping aside the dry earth. An ear showed itself, a forehead, an eyebrow. Tarchon hesitated to dig any further. Had he disturbed the grave of some murdered man? Then he touched the scalp and felt it warm under his hand, and began to dig furiously, with rising horror and panic.

As soon as the eyes were unearthed, their lids opened. As soon as he uncovered the mouth, it spoke. "Hail, Tarchon. I have little to offer but knowledge, but raise me up and I shall share with you everything I know." It was a boy!

Though his hair was grey and he wore the careworn expression of an old man, Tages was no more than a child! He came to light like some hoard of treasure buried in time of war. Like a treasure chest he was full of precious things. Tarchon took him to the city and introduced him to the officers and senators of Rome: "This is Tages who has come to teach us wonders!"

"Why? Who is he? What family? Who is his father?" asked the senators, affronted by the suggestion that a boy could teach them anything they did not already know.

"My father is a genius," replied Tages in his high, creaking voice, "one of the guardian spirits who keep watch over you from the hour of your birth till the moment of your death. My grandfather is Jupiter himself." Cries of "Blasphemy!" rose to a hundred lips, but there was something so unnerving about those age-milky eyes in that childish face that they let him go on. "Just as I was buried in the ground, so the future lies hidden in the fabric of Nature. I am come to teach you how to uncover those secrets. Fetch scrolls and let the scribes write down all that I say!"

He told them how flocks of birds sometimes write the future on the paper sky. He showed them how lightning could point its finger at the truth and light it up for all to see. He taught them the magic days of the calendar which, like pillars in a temple, lend strength to the year. He told them which dates should be festival days and which gods should be honoured at those festivals, which rites best pleased the gods, which flowers smelt sweetest in Heaven as they burned on an altar. Everything Tages said, the scribes wrote down, and when one scroll was filled, they started on another.

He showed them how chickens grew secrets, like eggs, within their feathery little bodies, and how the truth could be plucked out of the entrails of birds, like fishes out of the sea. In this way a man could discover whether a day would bring success, whether a battle would bring victory, a wedding happiness. In short, Tages taught the Romans all the arts and mysteries of augury and divination.

Twelve books of secrets Tages dictated, and all the while he spoke, he grew older before their very eyes: more sere and colourless and frail. Each day, when he had finished speaking, he would walk out across the ploughed fields around Rome. One day he simply sank down out of sight.

Tarchon ran to the spot, thinking to find the boy had fainted. But the soil had swallowed Tages, as it swallows the rainfall and the dew, down again into the dark ground where all things begin and end.

A SHOT
IN THE DARK

ORION, DIANA AND APOLLO'S SPITE

*N*o brother and sister could have been more different than Apollo and Diana. For Apollo had mastery over the sun and was hot-blooded and passionate. His sister, like the moon she mastered, was all coldness and pallor. Whereas Apollo chased any and every female, Diana had no interest in men, no patience with Love. Though nightly she kissed the shepherd Endymion at the portals of dawn, she had no wish for him to wake and return her kisses.

"I shall never marry," she told her father, and Jupiter dared not contradict her, for which of the Immortals would want such a coldly solitary bride? He allowed her to remain single, accompanied only by her train of unmarried nymphs. Beating the night forests with flails of moonlight, they nightly set the game birds flying, the red stags running. Diana was content to hunt, and she hunted better than any man.

There were seven sisters called the Pleiades among her followers, each as pretty as the other. They loved their mistress and had no wish to marry. What is more, they knew the penalty if they so much as smiled at a man while in the service of the virgin goddess.

So when Orion the Hunter caught sight of them one day, and came after them, intrigued by their prettiness, the seven fled him as they would a bear.

Orion was very like a bear – the great bulk of his shoulders, his mop of black hair. He was immensely tall, built on the scale of a god – a giant almost – and, being a hunter, he was quick on his feet. The girls had to run their hardest to stay ahead of him. Their fright and flight upset Orion – he meant them no harm – so he ran all the faster, calling for them to stop: "Don't be afraid! Don't run away!"

But the girls kept running: "Save us, mistress! Save us!"

As Orion's outstretched fingers brushed flying hair, the seven outran the very crest of a hill, planting their little feet in the springy black turf of the night sky. Staring after them in astonishment, he watched the Pleiades diminish to the size of children, of flowers, of flower petals, as they ran into the distant dark.

So that was where Orion stood when Diana first saw him. Full of rage, fully intending to turn him into some blighted tree or hideous beast, she sprinted up to him, hands spread to make magic. But her glare turned to blushes as he smiled at her. She saw, for the first time, this matchless piece of mankind. With his bow across his back, his great swordbelt cinched low about his hips, and his face flushed from running, here stood the greatest living hunter, a match for even the immortal huntress. His dog Sirius ran up, panting and grinning, and plunged his nose into her hand, snuffing the familiar scent of hunting.

As Orion smiled at Diana, all thought of the seven sisters slipped from his mind, and he loved Diana as instantly and completely as she loved him. They fell into step together, no words spoken, no words needed. The Moon goddess had found her mate. Orion's dog whimpered a little at being left behind unnoticed, then ran to catch up.

Day and night the two hunted together, and often the moon remained bright in the sky long after the sun was up.

The sun. Golden chariot of Diana's brother.

Apollo drove at breakneck speed across the blue fields of day, eagle-eyed, watching every man and beast, every right and wrong, every house and temple and trickling stream. He ploughed up the shadows with blades of sunlight so as to see into every cranny. No secret stayed hidden long from Apollo: no pretty face, dappled deer, no shady trickery, no lovers' tryst. He was brash and inquisitive, jealous of any happiness that was not his. He was arrogant and vain, too, and as spiteful as sunlight in a mirror.

When he saw Diana and Orion together, he laughed with disbelief at first, then with scorn. "What's this? My haughty sister who claims to despise all men so utterly? Holding hands with a mortal? What would our father Jupiter say, who granted you permission to stay single?" A hot, nagging pain just below his ribs made Apollo grind his teeth. Too proud to recognise the pangs of jealousy, he called it outrage. "You must be taught a lesson, sister. You must learn not to say one thing and do another!"

So Apollo kept watch until Diana was alone and walking on the foothills of Heaven. She was too thoughtful and happy even to quarrel with her brother when he chanced along in his loud yellow tunic and golden sandals.

"Our father was talking this morning of a contest among the gods," said Apollo blithely. "An Olympiad for Olympians. I said I would win every laurel."

"You might," Diana conceded generously. "Except for archery, of course."

"Archery? Why? Who could beat me at archery? Boy Cupid?"

"I could, naturally." Diana folded her arms.

"You? Beat me? Huh!"

Diana frowned and stamped one foot. "Everyone knows I am the best bar one—" She broke off, thinking better of naming Orion. He was her dear secret. "Bar none," she corrected herself.

"Huh!" snorted Apollo. "Why, with better light I could shoot that speck in the ocean and sink it." He pointed out across a sea purpling in the twilight. Far, far out, halfway to the horizon, a tiny dark speck bobbed on the waves: a seagull or a piece of driftwood.

"And I say I could hit it even in this light!" retorted Diana. "I can hit black boar in thickets of ebony at midnight." Stringing her bow in one smooth movement, Diana aimed an arrow at the distant fleck on the ocean …

Out beneath the first stars of evening, his dark hair spreading out from his head, Orion let the cool salt ocean wash away the dust and sweat of the day. He imagined swimming in the navy sky, where stars floated like little white fish and the Milky Way made a reef of white water. He thought of Diana, lovely Diana – of her brown fingers on the bowstring, of her soft footfall among the forest twigs … There was a thrumming hum in the purpling air, but he did not think 'arrows', did not think 'death'. He thought a shooting star must be falling towards him out of the sky …

When the arrow struck him in the throat, his dark eyes widened momentarily and he threw back his head, so that he glimpsed the seven little sisters, small as flower petals, huddling together at the far end of Night. Then the sea closed over his face, and the next wave rolled him over to float face down and dead.

"I shall never forgive you, Apollo," said Diana when she found out what she had done. Her brother sniggered and shrugged, but he found that the pain beneath his ribs had grown to an ache of regret. He had never seen his sister's face so ashy pale, never seen tears fall so fast from a face. "I swear I shall never forgive you," she said.

Apollo tossed his head with an arrogant, what-do-I-care swagger, and whipped his chariot horses to a gallop. But when he passed through the gates of sunset and glanced back at the night, he saw his sister dragging her lover behind her chariot like a victorious warrior dragging a vanquished opponent. She dragged Orion's body behind her silver chariot, up into the sky, while the dog Sirius ran howling behind. At the sky's zenith, she let Orion go, and his great form dissolved into fragments of light, expanding larger and larger until a starlight giant stood on the fields of night. His dog, too, she exploded into stars.

"You must keep him company now," Diana told Sirius. "Help him to watch over the Earth from now till the stars blow away." Pausing only to buckle round Orion's hips a new swordbelt of stars, she whipped up her own chariot and drove on towards dawn.

The seven sisters joined hands and danced in a ring to think that, now the danger was passed, Diana would fetch them down again to rejoin her train. But though they called out to her, they were too far off to make her hear, and Diana's mind was fixed on other things.

They are there even now, the seven sisters, the Pleiades. So, too, is Orion the Hunter, though he never glances their way. Nor does he even turn his head to see the Moon drive by. There is no heart beating, you see, in the hollow expanse of his chest. He is a constellation, untroubled by love or loneliness, heat or cold, trickery or sorrow. And he cuts such a gigantic figure, framed by Infinity, that Apollo, driving by in his golden chariot, looks no bigger than a bee buzzing through the grass at his feet.

THE GUARDIAN GEESE

THE NIGHT THE GAULS ATTACKED

Silent as worms, they burrowed under the walls of Veii. Their faces caked black with Etruscan earth, they scraped and scoured and clawed out soil, passing it back down the tunnel in willow baskets. The city had withstood their catapults and their battering rams, their siege ladders and their fire barrels. So now they were going in underground, to capture the prize Camillus had always dreamed of capturing. Veii was crammed with Etruscan treasure, and the general who could seize it would surely earn the undying gratitude of Rome!

In the darkest hour, his engineers broke through. They surfaced through the very floor of Juno's temple – and froze, mouths agape. "What is it? An ambush?" Camillus crawled past them impatiently, poking out his head through the broken planks of the floor.

He was confronted by a monumental, ghostly figure. The goddess Juno towered over him, fully seven metres tall, her eyes seeming to fasten on him with a queenly glare. It took him a moment to realize that it was only a statue. "O Juno! Queen of all the Gods! Forgive me that I enter your temple so rudely, without priests, without offerings. But smile on us this night and I swear that I shall clothe you in silk, house you in a finer temple by far, and set flocks of geese to guard you through the lonely night."

The statue's marble face expressed nothing, of course.

Out of the tunnel behind him, Camillus's legionaries crept one by one until they filled every alcove of the temple. Quietly they unbolted its great doors. Camillus raised his sword in salute to the goddess, then led them out on to the streets to surprise the Etruscans in their beds.

Veii fell overnight. Its treasures filled every cart in the city, and, all day long, cargoes of silver plate and shields, parchments and saddles, amphoras of wine and bolts of dyed cloth rolled out of the gates and away down the road towards Rome: booty for the victorious. Camillus was revelling in the sight, watching from the city walls, when his men came to him, trembling and tongue-tied. "Don't be angry, sir; it was maybe just the light, sir – a trick of the light, sir, but all of us felt it and we daren't go back in!" They were frightened of their general, but something in the temple of Juno had frightened them even more.

"Just tell me what happened," said Camillus.

"Well, we were washing her – like you ordered, sir! Washing and dressing her. She was covered in cobwebs, and what she was wearing before – well, it was no better than rags – a wicked disgrace, like you said. But then all of a sudden, sir, we couldn't, sir. We just somehow – no saying in words, sir – we just ... we just couldn't."

Camillus sighed. Superstitious soldiers could be an infernal nuisance. As he hurried to the temple, he saw the cart-horses outside trembling between the shafts: trembling and snorting and backing away. A whole detachment of soldiers hovered around the temple door, like men in a trance. But no sooner did he step inside than he understood what had frightened them and the horses. The statue, clean now and dressed in silk, had a quality of holiness about it which made the breath catch in his throat.

Falling on one knee, he bent his head. "O Juno, Bride of Jupiter,

87

Mother of Vulcan, Mistress of Heaven! Is it your wish to go to Rome, and is it I who shall have the honour of escorting you there?"

A soldier dropped his spear. A length of silk slithered to the ground. The great marble figure – every man there saw it – *dipped her head* in a gracious nod and closed her sightless white eyes. "You may," she seemed to say. "I consent. I am ready."

It was such a sight as stuck in each man's mind till the hour of his death. They laid her in the cart as though they were laying down a sleeping child, and when they reached Rome, each man bought, out of his own salary, a goose to loose in the temple of Juno.

High on the slopes of Heaven, Juno smiled to see the welcome Rome gave to her marble likeness. She smiled to see the thankful sacrifices offered up to her by devout, honourable Camillus (who kept all his promises). She smiled to see the geese, her sacred birds, waddle flat-footedly around the temple precincts like busy, officious little priests. At every honk, citizens turned their heads and looked towards the temple of Juno, remembering to praise the Queen of Immortals. She even smiled to see the doors of Janus's temple closed as the people of Rome put war behind them.

Without a war to fight, however, Rome thought she could do without her generals. Camillus, who had been welcomed home from Veii with garlands and speeches and gifts, was pensioned off, sent to live in the country, far away from the city. He went, but as he went he said, "Beware, Rome. Beware the Gauls! The Gauls have set their hearts on Rome."

The Gauls? Why would anyone fear the Gauls? Those uncivilised louts, oafish as bears? The Romans looked about them at their city, their empire, cultured and sophisticated, prosperous and elegant. How could a pack of tribal peasants, grubbing a living on the edge of the world, pose a threat to Rome?

The Gauls were indeed as savage as brute beasts: as hungry as well.

They were hungry for the treasures of Rome, just as Rome had been for the treasures of Veii. Like wolves drawn by the smell of cooking, they closed in from all sides until, one day, the people of Rome looked out and saw their eyes gleaming in the dark.

"Camillus! Where is Camillus?" they asked as the Gauls roared in at the gates.

"Send for Camillus! Let him save us!" they cried, choking on the smoke from their homes burning.

"Too late! No one can save us now!" they wailed as they ran for high ground, for Capitol Hill, which rose like a castle keep above the burning city.

The paths up to Capitol Hill were winding and easy to defend. The Gauls, though they washed around the foot of the hill like a flood tide, could not reach the summit where the terrified people cowered in the temples of their gods.

"We can wait!" the barbarians bawled up, in their guttural, ugly language. "Come down and die, or stay up there and starve!" And they prowled the base of the hill, looking for an unprotected path, some secret way up.

A lad found hiding in a grain jar told them what they wanted to know. He thought he could buy his life with the information, but the Gauls killed him anyway, and trod him underfoot as they scrambled up the steeply zigzag path. The temples of Jupiter and Juno would be crammed with treasures, crowded with pretty women, stashed with the prized possessions carried to the safety of the holy hill. It would be as easy as cutting the liver from a chicken … and the liver was always the sweetest part …

They went up at night, when the besieged Romans would not be expecting them. They blacked their faces with earth and trod softly, so as to keep the advantage of surprise. Easier to slit the throats of sleepers than wait till they woke. The leading man could hear the snores of sleeping

Romans as he reached the summit, raised an arm, a knee, over a low stone parapet. There was a dagger clenched between his teeth.

Then a white demon reared up in his face: a white demon with an orange mask. It swamped him in a hissing roar, then drove its steel-hard face into his, cracking the bridge of his nose. The universe seemed to be full of these monstrous white harpies, blaring and stabbing, hammering on the Gauls with wings as hard as sail-booms. The men first over the wall fell back on to those behind them, dislodging them from the steep path and sending them hurtling down the side of Capitol Hill. The chorus of shrieking went on and on until every Imperial guard was awake, every dagger drawn. Mothers gathered their children into their arms, men drew their weapons, priests lit beacon fires to see by. The Gauls were driven off, nursing bloody noses and marvelling at what demons the Romans had tamed to guard their holy citadel.

They regrouped, of course, ready to rush the hill at dawn …
but dawn found Camillus standing in the ashes of the city gates,
a cohort of soldiers close-ranked behind him. The Gauls were
trapped like rabbits in the last sheaf of corn.

Once more Camillus was garlanded and fêted and cheered
through the streets, though now the noble buildings lay in ruins
and the air reeked of smoke. Once again the altar of Juno was
heaped with flowers and fruit, while prayers of thanksgiving rose
up to Heaven. But the greatest reward went to Juno's sacred
geese. Poured out in golden torrents, splashing on to the
pavements of the temple, rattling around their paddling, in-turned
feet, whole bushels of corn were scattered for the marvellous
birds who had saved Rome's holy places from the enemy. Even
the huge, serene statue of the goddess, Queen of the Gods,
seemed to smile down fondly at the funny, fussy creatures,
while the geese themselves swung their rear ends with a
new swagger, honking as if to say, "Make way! Make way!
Maaaake way!"

THE GODS AND GODDESSES OF ROME

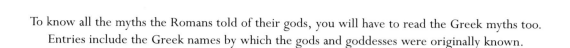

To know all the myths the Romans told of their gods, you will have to read the Greek myths too. Entries include the Greek names by which the gods and goddesses were originally known.

APOLLO, god of music, archery, sports and prophecy. The son of Jupiter and brother of Diana, he was often thought of as the sun god, and therefore as important and powerful as Jupiter himself. (Greek: Apollo)

CERES, goddess of vegetation and fruitfulness. The word 'cereal' derives from her name. (Greek: Demeter)

CUPID, son of Mars and Venus. (Greek: Eros)

DIANA, goddess of woodlands, the moon and hunting; she also protected expectant mothers. (Greek: Artemis)

DIS, a name for the Underworld, and also the god of the Underworld, known to the Greeks as Pluto. Though gloomy and sad, it was not a place of torment and punishment.

JANUS, a uniquely Roman god with two faces, looking both ways. He was not only god of doorways, but of New Year, when people look to both future and past.

JUPITER, King of the Gods, Optimus Maximus (the best and greatest). His other names hint at his various roles: Thunderer, Shaker of Lightning, Supreme Commander, The Triumphant One, Winner of Battle Spoils. (Greek: Zeus)

JUNO, wife of Jupiter, Queen of the Gods, goddess of marriage and fertility – not so quarrelsome as her Greek counterpart, Hera. Her month (June) was thought the luckiest for weddings.

LARES, a lar was a household god – according to myth, an invisible child of Lara and Mercury, but commonly thought of, too, as the spirit of a family ancestor.

LIBER, an ancient Italian god of the countryside and of wine, different from the Greek Dionysus who also appears among the Roman gods.

MARS, the god of war. Born of Juno without the aid of Jupiter, he was a favourite god of the warlike Romans. His month, March, brought the start of the campaigning season. (Greek: Aries)

MERCURY, god of trade (especially corn) and, like Hermes, his Greek counterpart, messenger to the gods. The liquid metal quicksilver was named 'mercury' after him, because of his speed of movement.

MINERVA, goddess of wisdom, the arts and of handicrafts, born directly out of Jupiter's head. Like her Greek counterpart Athena, she often wore armour and displayed a warlike nature.

NEPTUNE, god of water, but much less important than the Greek Poseidon.

SATURN, an ancient Italian god of agriculture. His temple in Rome served as the treasury and his December festival, the Saturnalia, was a week-long riotous party, a forerunner of our Christmas celebrations. Saturday is named after him. (Greek: Kronos)

VENUS, goddess of spring and of love who supposedly helped her mortal son Aeneas throughout his life. (Greek: Aphrodite)

VESTA, goddess of hearth and home and protector of the Roman nation as well as the Vestal Virgins, she is much more important than her Greek counterpart Hestia.

VULCAN, is the blacksmith god who makes thunderbolts for Jupiter at his forge under the volcano Etna. (Greek: Hephaestus)

NOTES ABOUT THE STORIES

The Olympians

Even after the home of the gods ceased to be thought of as Mount Olympus and became, instead, the sky itself, the gods of the upper world were known as the Olympians. It distinguished them from the gods of the Underworld. Jupiter is generally depicted in art seated on a throne holding Victoria in the palm of his hand. Homer's original recounting of Ganymede's story was added to by later writers with details such as Jupiter's disguise as an eagle and the placing of Ganymede on Mount Ida.

In the night sky, the constellation of Aquarius represents Ganymede carrying wine to the gods.

Chains of Love

On a Roman bride's wedding day, she would cut off a lock of hair and sacrifice it to Venus, goddess of love. Venus is supposed to have loved, at various times, Mars, Bacchus, Mercury, Neptune, Anchises and Adonis. But her marriage to Vulcan makes better sense than appears at first sight: Venus, being the mother of Aeneas, was tremendously important to the Romans, but so too was Vulcan. His temple was considered to be the centre-point of the whole Roman state, founded by Romulus.

Dreams of Destiny / To Hell and Back

It is impossible to do justice, in two short chapters, to the epic *Aeneid* by Virgil. In the space of twelve books he traces Roman civilisation back to Troy. After the fall of Troy, its hero, Aeneas, embarks on a long, eventful journey, by way of Carthage and the Underworld, before doing battle for the hand of Lavinia, his wife, and settling in Latium, the region to be inhabited by his 'Roman' descendants. Virgil died in 19 BC, before this huge work was complete. It was commissioned by Octavius (Augustus) Caesar and was hugely welcomed, because of the sense of national pride it encouraged.

Romulus and Remus

There are two different endings to this story. One says that Romulus, as first ruler of Rome, grew to be such a tyrant that his own senators stabbed him, cut him in pieces and hid the pieces under their cloaks, telling the gullible people that he had been snatched away by the gods. The other says that he died gloriously in battle, Jupiter allowing Mars to come down and carry Romulus home in his chariot. He was worshipped as a god in Rome, under the name of Quirinius.

Stolen Wives

The Sabines were the most ancient and most powerful Italian tribe absorbed into the Roman Empire. They were renowned for their virtue, bravery, their honourable and religious nature and the value they placed on freedom. According to legend, after the theft of their wives and daughters, they united with the Romans under a general called Quirites.

A Wild Goose Chase

The oath which Jupiter swears, granting Philemon and Baucis anything they request, is the most solemn pledge any Roman could make: he swears by the Styx, the river flowing between the world of the Living and the land of the Dead. The recurrence of this theme of the good host – (see *Liber-ality*) – shows what great store was set by hospitality.

Liber-ality

Liber was, in fact, an Italian god of wine long before the Greek god Dionysus was imported and worshipped under the name of Bacchus. He had a female counterpart, too, called Libera. Their festival – the Liberalia – was held each year on 17 March (a strange time of year considering that the wine harvest falls in late summer). Falerno, a sweet wine still produced north of Naples, was the favourite drink of the Romans. The great poet Horace even wrote verse in praise of it. It takes its name, of course, from Falernus.

Kissed by the Moon

It is thought now that the myth of Endymion and Diana is really about the sun and moon: Diana the moon and Endymion the setting sun. Apparently, in ancient times, people used to use expressions such as "Diana loves and watches Endymion" to say "It's getting late." "Diana has sent Endymion to sleep with her kisses" meant "It's night-time."

The story has always been popular with poets: John Keats, for example, wrote a long version in verse.

The Man Who Cut Down Trees

In all cultures, clumps of ancient trees have inspired religious awe. In Rome, certain oak groves were sacred to Ceres, goddess of vegetation. It is easy to imagine how some free-thinking unbeliever might have made fun of this superstitious tree-worship, then, to everyone's spiteful delight, come to a sticky end. Another tells how Ceres threw gruel into the face of a boy who laughed at her, and turned him into a lizard.

Tell Tale Tit

Every house in Rome had its Lares and Penates – little statues made of clay, wax, ivory, silver or gold, depending how rich the family was. Every mealtime, a little food would be placed in a bowl in front of the Penates. In return, these household gods would ensure domestic happiness. The Lares stood on the family hearth: statues looking like fur-coated monkeys with barking dogs at their feet. They guarded the house.

Lares and Penates are an entirely Roman phenomenon, unknown to the Greeks.

Burning the Books

These mysterious books really were preserved in Rome and, whenever danger threatened, read by the Senate, in search of advice. At first, the three volumes were stored in a stone chest, under the floor of Jupiter's Capitol temple, cared for by fifteen specially chosen guardians. Caesar Augustus then edited out two thousand verses, encased the rest in gold, and buried them under Apollo's statue on the Palatine Hill. When the city burned down, during the reign of Nero, the last of the Sibylline prophecies were destroyed.

Little Old Boy

Tarchon is the Moses of Etruscan myth; he led his tribe out of Libya during a famine, and settled them in present-day Tuscany, founding the city of Tarquinia. He also helped Aeneas. Fortune-tellers were much relied on by the superstitious Romans. This myth helps lend mystical authority to those priestly practitioners who read omens in the internal organs (augurs) of chickens. The complicated rituals of augury were known as 'The Haruspices'.

A Shot in the Dark

Orion's story is a long one, involving a string of women. Before meeting Diana, he was pursuing her entire train of nymphs, the Pleiades. In order to escape, they turned first into seven white doves, then into a cluster of stars. Orion consoled himself with Princess Merope of Chios but, for the crime of eloping with her, was blinded and left to stumble in misery through the world until the sun shone in his face and restored his sight. It is fitting, even so, that his eternal companion in the night sky is not a woman but Sirius his dog; Orion's first love was hunting.

The Guardian Geese

Each of the gods had particular animals which were sacred to them. In the case of Juno, it was geese, and, since Juno's temple was on the Capitoline Hill, there would certainly have been geese wandering about on the hilltop. In 390 BC the Gauls attacked Rome and all but destroyed it. Afterwards, to commemorate the part played by Juno's geese in alerting the sentries, a golden goose was carried in procession every year up to the Capitol.